YOUR MIND
is Like a
Garden

'To Roger... with thanks for our
mindful moments together.'
– Shona Innes

'To the great mind gardener Shona.'
– Írisz Agócs

Five Mile, an imprint of
Bonnier Publishing Australia
Level 6, 534 Church Street,
Richmond, Victoria 3121
www.fivemile.com.au

First published 2017
Printed in China 5 4 3 2 1

YOUR MIND is Like a Garden

Shona Innes * Írisz Agócs

FIVE MILE

Our mind is a brilliant and clever thing.

Our mind is our very own.

We can't see or touch someone's mind, but everyone has one busily working away inside them.

Our mind thinks, works out stuff, feels, listens,
watches and tells us things.

Our mind can get very busy.
Sometimes our mind gets too
busy and it can get stuck.

Sometimes when our mind is busy we
can feel upset or confused.
It can be hard to think, or get to sleep
or get ready to learn and do things
that make us happy.

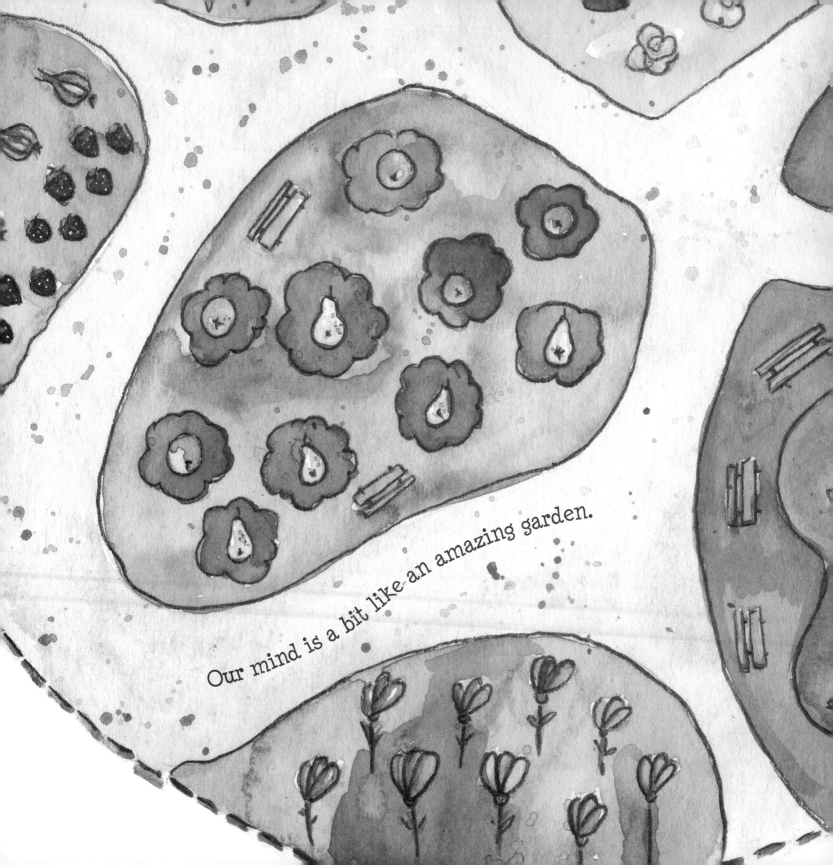

Our mind is a bit like an amazing garden.

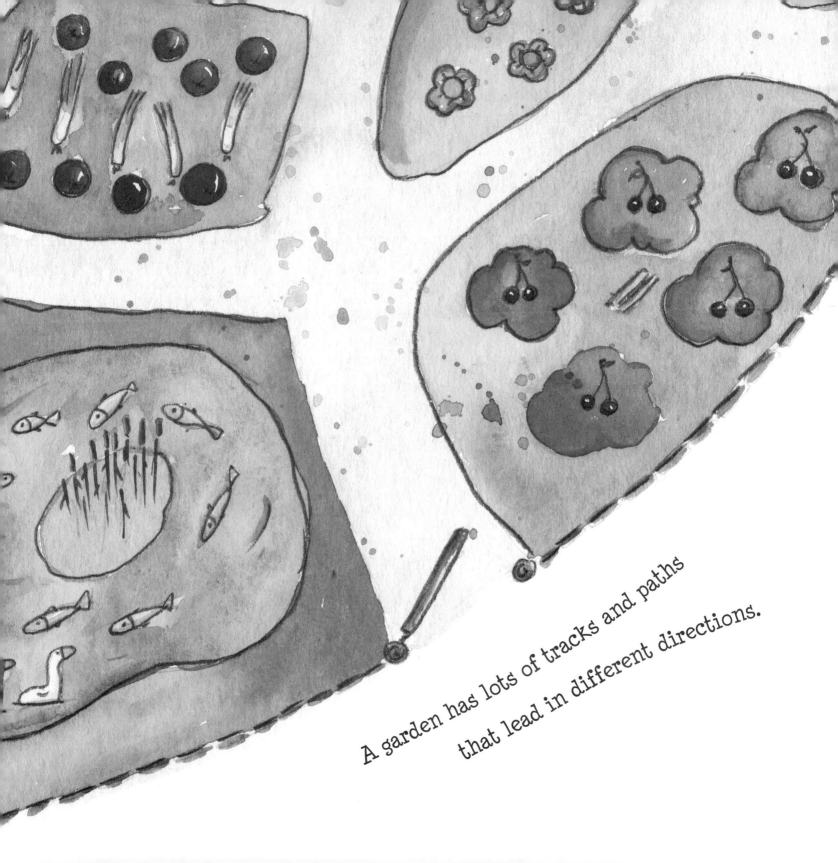

A garden has lots of tracks and paths that lead in different directions.

A garden has wide open spaces
where we can create and play.

It has places to grow things and do work.

A garden has lots of places to put things and store them for later.

Our mind is like a garden.

It has clever parts that help us to grow and learn.

It has places where we can create and have fun.

It has places to keep and remember things.

Our mind is always there, but sometimes we get too busy and we can forget about it.

Sometimes, it's lovely to just sit back and
watch the garden in our mind
— to sit still and close our eyes

and listen to the noises in our mind

and hear what our mind says to us.

To get back to our mind garden we need to be still for a while.
When we are still we can start to feel our belly
move slowly up and down as the air moves in and out of us.

We can feel the breath cool as we breathe in and warm, and
a bit wet, as we breathe out. If we are very still, we can listen to
the sound our breathing makes.

If we stay very quiet a little longer,

we might be able to hear or see our mind garden.

We might hear or see our mind's thoughts popping up

like flowers in a garden.

There might be lots of them, or just one or two.

We don't have
to do anything
with our thought
flowers,

just watch them quietly and know they are there.

Thoughts usually grow one at a time but sometimes
they can grow really quickly.
Sometimes we get so caught up watching one
thought we might miss the others.

If we get stuck on a thought or caught on one thing in our mind, we can just remind ourself to let that one go and sit back and watch for the next ones.

When we have watched the thoughts growing in our mind garden, we can make ourselves still and calm.

When we are ready, we can come back to listen to our breath again and the sounds of the world around us.

Our mind is always there.
We can visit it and watch the
thoughts it grows any time.

When we visit our mind garden we can make our minds less busy.

Calm and wonderful!